HOW TO DO CONTENT MARKETING

BUSINESS SKILLS FOR EDITORS: 1

Louise Harnby

ISBN: 9798668542895

CONTENTS

1. Introduction

Overview

Content marketing has been an integral part of my promotion strategy since I launched my editorial business in 2006. Why do I do it? Why might you do it?

Ultimately, like any element of a marketing strategy, it's about increasing the discoverability of our businesses so that we have choice in the fees we accept or set, the clients we work for and the number of hours we dedicate to that work.

What's included

In this guide, I'll take you through the basics of content marketing. First, we'll consider what it is and take a look at some industry definitions. I'll offer you a simple starter definition to make the journey more accessible. Then we'll look more closely at value (usefulness), and how this needs to underpin every piece of content marketing you carry out.

Second, we'll take a look at the various different types of content that you might consider creating for your own strategy, and some fabulous examples of content marketing in action – value that our fellow editors and proofreaders have already created and delivered to a specific customer or client.

Third, I'll offer you a simple framework on which to construct your own content marketing. I've included a couple of case studies that use this framework. You can copy them and use them to help you build your own valuable content, with the help of the template in the appendix.

Fourth, we'll look at timing and branding – when to create content and what it should look like so that it puts your best business-face forward.

And, finally, we'll revisit the industry definitions and use the information offered throughout the guide to unravel any sticking points.

The power of content

Content marketing can feel like a chore to the inexperienced marketer and new business owner. However, it's one of the most powerful tools available for connecting and engaging with fellow editorial professionals and potential clients. Furthermore, it continues to deliver, time and time again. When you create great content that meets the criteria outlined in this guide, you'll generate benefits for your business not just now but for years to come.

2. Content marketing and your business goals

Overview

Why bother with a content-marketing strategy? The answer is simple – it can help us to meet our business goals. You and I might have very different goals. Furthermore, those goals might change over time because our professional and personal circumstances change. Having choice puts us in a position where we can better adapt to those changes.

Business goals

Start by thinking about what your business goals are. Here are some ideas to help you structure your thinking.

Acquire clients

If you're in the early phase of your editorial career, you'll want to begin the process of being visible as quickly as possible. Content marketing isn't by any means the only way of promoting your business to acquire clients, but it's one way.

Acquire different types of clients

Changes in the market may be affecting your workflow negatively. For example, let's say you work primarily with academic publishers. Some have begun to insist that their authors source copyediting or proofreading for their books and journals, thus reducing the supply of work available. Content marketing could, over time, provide you with access to these authors in the open market, and to completely new client groups.

Increase income

Perhaps you need to increase the amount you earn to meet a change in circumstances (e.g. increase in family size). Content marketing could, over time, provide you with access to less price-sensitive markets that allow you to work fewer hours for a higher hourly rate.

Develop additional income streams

Not all of your content needs to be free. Some of your content could be charged for (e.g. a book, a course, a speaking engagement). This would provide you with an additional income to supplement your editorial business earnings.

Explore new opportunities

You might wish to gradually expand your business into new areas (e.g. training, speaking). Content marketing can facilitate this expansion because, through it, you create a bank of value that presents you as a credible thought leader in your field.

Whatever content you create, and whomever you create it for, keep your business goals in mind so that you stay focused on ensuring that the time you invest in creating and delivering the additional value is moving you towards reaching them.

3. What is content marketing?

Overview

First off, I have a confession. I don't like the term 'content marketing'. There are a couple of reasons for this:

- The term itself omits the very word that underpins its premise – that word is *value*.
- Some of the definitions provided by the content-marketing industry verge on impenetrable for the inexperienced editorial marketer.

Industry definitions

Let's take a look at a couple of those industry definitions. They might seem a little daunting now but they'll be useful to refer back to at the end of the guide:

> Content marketing is a strategic marketing approach focused on creating and distributing valuable, relevant, and consistent content to attract and retain a clearly-defined audience – and, ultimately, to drive profitable customer action. (Content Marketing Institute)

> Content marketing is the discipline of creating quality branded editorial content across all media channels and platforms to deliver engaging relationships, consumer value and measurable success for brands. (Content Marketing Association)

If you're new to marketing, terms like 'customer action', 'consumer value' and 'measurable success' might have you reaching for something stronger than lemonade.

With that in mind, I'd like to offer you something a little simpler to start with:

Content marketing = creating and delivering useful stuff

If content is useful, it's valuable. And value is everything. If the person at whom the content is targeted sees no intrinsic value in what you've created, at best they won't remember you or your business; at worst, they'll be actively put off.

Focusing on value is therefore essential and it's for that reason that I often refer to it by a different name – value-added marketing.

For whom is content valuable?

Content marketing starts with the customer – that is, the person at whom the content is targeted.

As editorial freelancers, we have two primary customer groups:

- **Colleagues** who can recommend our editorial services if their own schedules are too busy or if they believe we have more relevant specialist skills. They might also buy relevant paid-for content.
- **Clients** who hire our proofreading and editing services. They might also refer our services to their own contacts.

Even within these customer groups, there'll be differences in what's considered valuable. My clients include self-publishing authors, students, businesses and publishers. Not all my client-focused content will appeal to all of those subgroups.

Furthermore, you might wish to create content that's targeted at specific sub-subgroups – legal students, independent fiction authors, science scholars.

Putting the audience front of mind

When we create and deliver useful stuff, we need to have the customer front of mind, otherwise the content might not be pitched right or might not solve their problems. If the pitch is wrong, the customer could disengage because they don't understand how the content relates to their needs. And if the content doesn't solve the customer's problems, it's not useful and is therefore of no value.

Building good relationships, especially when the audience is one whom we've not met before (e.g. a potential new client), requires instilling trust in them. Coming across as authentic and honest is therefore important. Care needs to be taken, though. We need to strike a balance – self-reflection that offers solutions rather than self-reflection that doesn't.

When solutions are absent, the content becomes all about the creator when it should be about the customer. If a blog article, podcast or presentation is ultimately about the customer, it's a content-marketing piece. If it's ultimately about the creator, it's an opinion piece. There's nothing wrong with creating opinion pieces, but because they're not solution-focused they're less likely to help us reach our business goals.

4. Working out what's useful and visible

Overview

Once you've identified your customer, ask yourself what their problems are and how you might provide useful stuff that will put you top of mind (or top of the search engines) when they source a proofreader or editor.

Sourcing problems through questions

If you don't know what your customers' problems are, follow Martin Huntbach's advice in '7 Ways Content Marketing will Improve Search Engine Optimisation':

> [T]ake note of what your customers ask you. I've gained so many content ideas just from the questions my clients have asked. If they're asking, I'd bet a lot of others are too.

Below are some questions that customers (clients and colleagues) often ask. The answers to these have already been provided, or will be in the future, by editorial professionals via visible, value-adding content.

All we have to do is listen to the questions we're being asked, and then get busy delivering the answers.

- How do you format a bibliography using APA style?
- What's a vocative comma and how do I use it?
- What are the best style manuals to use when editing or proofreading fiction?
- How do I get started in editorial freelancing?
- What's a good rate of pay?
- Should I publish in print or digital?
- What's a manuscript critique?
- How do I use Track Changes in Word?

- How much does copyediting or proofreading cost and which service do I need?

And, remember, there's no one way to provide value – the content that your target customer will engage with can take multiple forms. Here are just a few examples of how you might offer something useful to a client or colleague:

- Teach a skill (e.g. Microsoft Word Styles tutorial)
- Affirm current practice (e.g. how to proofread onscreen)
- Offer solutions (e.g. information about productivity enhancement)
- Demonstrate a tool (e.g. a macro)
- Encourage other ways of thinking (e.g. different strategies for increasing editorial freelancing rates)
- Share wisdom and experience (e.g. via a blog)

Top of Google and top of mind

Being top of mind and top of Google are not the only ways of generating an editorial work stream, but they're not to be ignored if you want to maximize your choice.

Top of Google (and other search engines)

Being visible online is essential in today's editorial freelancing market.

Some client types are easy to make oneself visible to – publishers, for example. Proofreaders and editors are a conventional part of the book and journal production workflow. As such, all it takes to make first contact is a letter or email with accompanying CV. However, you might find that the fees on offer from this client group don't meet your minimum price requirements or your maximum price goals.

Corporate clients and independent authors might be a better price match for you. Being visible to these types of clients, such that enough of them contact you on a regular basis to fill your schedule and provide you with your desired income, is a harder nut to crack. Discoverability through the search engines (SEO) is a must.

Content marketing is an important part of any SEO strategy. Why? Essentially, it boils down to the following:

- Google rewards websites that are regularly updated with fresh, original content
- Google rewards websites whose content is shared
- Google rewards websites whose content is linked to by relevant websites, and which themselves link to other relevant websites (inbound and outbound links)

When you create useful stuff, and share that useful stuff with an audience who finds value in it, they in turn share it and link to it. Google thinks you're interesting and rewards you with higher rankings. That in turn means you're easier to find for certain keyword searches by potential clients.

Top of mind

Being top of mind relates both to clients and to colleagues. Here, your content presents you as an expert in a particular field. Then, when a client or colleague needs to find a proofreader or editor, you spring to mind.

Example

Perhaps you're a specialist legal editor and you've created and uploaded a tutorial on how to format references according to OSCOLA (Oxford Standard for Citation of Legal Authorities) style to your website and your YouTube channel. You share a link to the editorial community via your networking channels.

Your demo will be useful to, for example, first-year legal students. One of them uses Google to search for 'OSCOLA video' and your content shows up in the listing. The student finds your video useful, and returns to it often when she's stuck. A year later, she's preparing to submit her Master's dissertation. She's advised by her supervisor to source a professional proofreader to polish the language. It's yet another thing to add to her already busy to-do list.

But hang on a minute, she thinks. Guess who's top of mind? That afternoon, an email drops into your inbox, requesting a quote for legal proofreading services.

One of your colleagues is a specialist fiction editor. A potential client contacts her about proofreading a paper that will be submitted to a legal journal. Your colleague remembers the information you shared about OSCOLA, knows you'd be a better fit for the client, and sends the author your email address.

Being human

One of the best things about great content marketing is that it's all about being a normal human being, and it therefore comes naturally to us ... well, most of us! Have a gander at the following list. Do any of the items strike you as things you're capable of doing?

- Being friendly – engaging with people in a respectful and approachable manner
- Being interesting – a good friend who gives as well as takes
- Sharing things of value to those who you're hanging out with
- Listening/engaging as well as talking
- Responding with curiosity before judgement

It wouldn't surprise me if you answered yes to the entire list. Here's the thing – people who behave like that are usually well liked by others in the world. They are rewarded with friends, acquaintances and colleagues who speak well of them and support them. If you can do that in the business world, you've got yourself a network.

Google's not so different and it's one of the things I like best about it. It doesn't matter how rich you are, what class you are, what your sexual preferences are or how you identify in terms of ethnicity. If Google thinks others find you interesting because they're sharing stuff of value that you've created, it'll reward you with higher rankings. It'll reward you for behaving like a normal human being.

Content marketing allows you to market your business in a way that harnesses what you do naturally. And it's recommended by experts. Here's Donna Moritz, a visual marketing specialist, with one of her predictions for effective content marketing ('25 Experts Share Top 3 Content Marketing Trends for 2017'):

> More than ever we will need to be 'human' in our marketing as fans want to know the people behind the brand.

5. Different types of content marketing

Overview

There are lots and lots of ways of doing content marketing. If you think that content marketing is only about the digital environment, or only about video, you're mistaken. The digital and the visual are hugely important, given that so many people use the internet, but they're not the only ways of delivering useful stuff, and won't be as long as there are audiences who operate in non-digital environments.

The thing is, people were content marketing before Tim Berners-Lee was born – perhaps they didn't use that term to describe what they were doing, but that's what it was all the same.

The different types of content

The list below might surprise you – after reviewing it, you'll probably realize you've being creating and delivering added value without even knowing it!

- Infographics
- Video tutorials, screencasts, demos and interviews
- Downloadable templates (e.g. style sheet, excel formula, accounts schedule)
- Blogs – advice, screenshot-based demos
- Podcasts (audio)
- Information leaflets, checklists and cheat-sheets
- Booklets and books
- Apps, tools and widgets
- Knowledge hubs
- Presentations – in-room and remote (e.g. conference vs recorded webinar)
- Training courses – on-site and remote (e.g. on-site vs interactive webinar)

- Business-related forums (online) and meet-ups (conferences)
- Conversations with colleagues and friends

What can be defined as content marketing is actually rather broad – which is great because it means that even the most inexperienced marketers have probably already done some of it.

Remember, if the conversation, the forum discussion, the blog or the tool is considered useful and valuable to the person it's targeted at, then it's contributing to moving you to top of mind (or top of Google), and that means it's working as a form of content marketing.

The digital environment

Having said above that content marketing goes beyond the digital, you'd be bonkers not to embrace the online environment if you're serious about incorporating valuable content creation into your broader marketing strategy.

Being online provides unprecedented opportunities for delivery, and while your audience might prefer text for X, audio for Y, and video for Z, you can offer all of these things in a digital environment, and you can reach the widest number of people.

6. The underlying principles of content marketing

Overview

There are some basic principles that must underpin effective content marketing.

Understanding these will help to take you beyond my initial simplistic definition of content marketing so that the value-adding content you create helps to drive you towards the business goals you've identified (e.g. increased income, client acquisition, being in a position to take advantage of opportunities).

We've already discussed the first, value. I hope you can see why I've placed it right at the top of the graphic below.

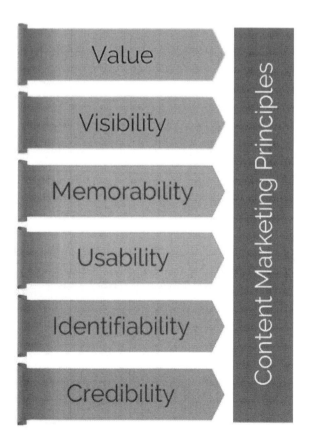

Value

To recap, value is everything. Content must be of use to the person it's targeted at – your audience. Content that has no value will not be shared, talked about, recommended or linked to. If it's not shared, talked about, recommended and linked to, it won't move you and your business to the top of people's minds or the top of the search engines, which means it won't serve to increase the chance of a work lead coming your way.

Web strategist and marketer Aaron Agius, in '25 Experts Share Top 3 Content Marketing Trends for 2017', recommends thinking in terms of 'personalisation'. This means producing:

> … content that is created and focussed as much as possible on specific people and personas. This allows the content to be of as much value as possible to the readers.

If you think you might forget to focus on value, don't call this activity content marketing. Call it **value-added marketing**. That way, the terminology you're using will serve to remind you of what's important.

Visibility

If your content's invisible, you've wasted your time creating it.

Let's imagine that you're an experienced medical editor – you know the training required and who the industry-recognized providers are; you know the kinds of clients who use medical editors and where to source them; you have a realistic appreciation of what rates might be commanded from various client groups within the field by medical editors with different levels of experience; and you understand the challenges confronting the medical editor and have sound advice on how to overcome them.

You create a PDF that summarizes all of your wisdom.

The problem is that no one knows it exists. You're not connected with an online community of editors, medical or otherwise. You don't have a Twitter account, a LinkedIn profile or a Facebook page. You're wary of online discussion groups and, so far, you've been too shy to attend your national editorial society's conference or chapter meetings. All of that means you have no way of communicating the fact that this amazing resource exists.

If you *were* connected with the resource's target audience, you'd be able to use those social media platforms and business networks to share a link to that PDF. And because it's such a great resource, people from your community would re-share that information, link to it, talk about it and recommend it. All of this would help to put you top of colleagues' minds as an experienced, go-to medical editor. And when a client comes calling who wants a medical editor, and a colleague isn't a medical editor, guess who they'll recommend to the client? You.

My colleague Katharine O'Moore-Klopf is an example of a medical editor who's nailed her content-marketing strategy perfectly. She's written about how to specialize in this field, but beforehand she'd developed the network through which to share this knowledge and make it visible.

Furthermore, all that linking and sharing contributes to Google's thinking you're interesting within a particular search framework (e.g. medical editing), so you're rewarded with a nudge up the search rankings. In other words, because your content's visible, you and your business are more visible.

Invisible content is not content marketing, however useful it is. It's just stuff. If you're not connected with your target audience, get connected in as many ways as you can. Join your national editorial society, build and use your social media networks, take part in forum discussions, meet people, talk, listen, engage.

Take note of who the key influencers are, who's active and engaged, who's talking about problems and offering solutions. This is what social media marketing consultant Mark Schaefer calls your 'Alpha Audience' (for more information, see 'Driving economic benefits from your Alpha Audience'). The Alpha Audience is made up of the people who are most likely to be 'passionate advocates' of the valuable content you create, and are therefore most likely to share it, recommend it and link to it.

Memorability

Is the content memorable? In other words, is it saying something new, or newish? There's nothing wrong with creating content that's already available in different forms elsewhere, but do put your own voice or angle on it. Try to find a way to enhance what's already out there so that your target audience has something new to gain by engaging with your content. That way, it'll be worth their time to share, talk about, link to and recommend it.

One of my colleagues, Liz Dexter, has produced some useful blog posts with screenshots that show clients and colleagues how to use Word's Styles palette. When another colleague, Kat Trail, decided to do the same, she created a video tutorial instead; also, she was demoing on a Mac rather than a PC.

Both these editors have created content that solves the same problem for the same audience but they do it in different ways, so both are memorable and useful.

Ultimately, if your content marketing is forgettable, so are you and your business.

Usability

Here, I'm talking about format or method of delivery. Effective content marketing needs to be accessible to – usable for – the audience at whom it's targeted (clients or colleagues).

In other words, we're putting the customer first. When the preferences of the customer are dismissed, we restrict who'll be able to access our content. This in turn restricts who'll talk about it, link to it, talk about it and share it. And that's restricting our ability to move to top of mind and top of Google.

There's a quotation from graphic-design guru Paul Rand that's all over the internet: 'Design is the silent ambassador of your brand.' I don't know whether Rand was talking purely in terms of the aesthetic when he said those words but, even if he was, I think there's a broader lesson there: if you haven't designed your content marketing pieces in a way that makes them accessible to, or usable for, the customer, then you're not doing yourself any favours.

When I launched my first editorial book, I made it available in eformat only, because that was what was convenient for me. However, I'd made a mistake. Many of my customers (colleagues in this case) wanted a paperback; a year later, I rectified the problem. Then colleagues began to ask whether they could buy both books in a package at a discounted price. My response?

Amazon won't let me do this. The issue here is that I was making it all about me. Instead, I should have got my act together more quickly and responded to what my customers wanted. In 2016, I launched the PDF omnibus, which includes both books and the bonus of some additional, related, material. Finally, I was offering what my customers had asked for.

Recall Martin Huntbach's excellent advice about working out what kind of content to create by *listening* to the questions that our customers ask. Both he and Rand remind us that *how* is as important as *what*.

If you want your content to reach the largest number of people who can engage with it, ask yourself what they want and how they want it.

- If most of your customers want to read an article, a podcast won't be the best way of communicating your message and putting yourself top of mind. Might you do both, though?
- If your content is complicated, might you support it with an infographic to increase engagement and consolidate the message you want to communicate?
- If you've provided an Excel template with complex formulae included, do you need to build in a supporting textual explanation on how to use it?
- If you've created a macro, are installation instructions required for novice users? Would a video tutorial be more effective than written instructions, or will both be better?

Content that isn't usable can end up as static – it doesn't go anywhere. It's therefore dead, at least to some members of your audience. Create it and deliver it in formats that your customers want rather than in ways that are simple and convenient for you.

Identifiability

Your content marketing material needs to look great *and* it needs to look like it's yours. That way, people can identify it with you and your business. We're talking about branding – not just a design brand, but a reputational one too.

Business first

Make sure it has your business name (and logo if you have one) on it. Whether it's a booklet, an infographic, a slide show, a checklist or a video, ensure your audience knows that it's you who created it.

If you're in a situation where the valuable content you'll be offering is in the form of a face-to-face conversation (e.g. you're presenting at conference, running a workshop, or attending a networking meeting to share advice and experience), business cards will be a must-have.

If you're engaging on professional forums, take care to include a signature so that your colleagues know who you are and how to get in touch.

Consistency of quality

Commission fellow editorial professionals to ensure it's in top-notch shape and reflects what you do as an editorial business owner. I hire a colleague to proofread my blog posts. I know that when I write I'm too close to my own content. Getting a fresh set of eyes on my writing makes sense – it's what I want my clients to do, so why wouldn't I follow the very example I set? The outlay is a tax-deductible expense, which keeps costs down.

Colourway or design

If you're producing multiple types of similar content, consider using a similar design for each piece. This helps customers to immediately recognize the content as something you've produced. Take a look at the following examples of my guides, books and freebies.

When your content is immediately identifiable, the trust and credibility you've built with your first or second pieces will transfer more easily to later ones. That means it's more likely to be talked about, shared, linked to and recommended.

Professionalism

Your content marketing should be branded with positivity and a solution-based focus. Put your best face forward. Clients and colleagues should review your content and be impressed with you, not feel sorry for you.

If you're having a tough time, by all means discuss it with trusted friends and colleagues, but do it in a private space – recognize the personal/professional divide. No client will feel compelled to hire someone who seems vulnerable. Or, if they do, they could feel that they're in a position to exploit your vulnerability by haggling over rates or turnaround times.

Remember, too, that our clients might feel vulnerable, particularly if they're, say, first-time writers, writing in a second language, or beginner academics. We're supposed to instil them with confidence in our ability to help them, not leave them wondering whether they're hiring someone whose head's in the wrong space.

Value, value, value

Don't forget that value is king when it comes to content marketing. If you're moaning instead of helping, then it's not useful to your colleagues. It may still put you top of mind, but for all the wrong reasons.

In effect, you'll be branding yourself (and your business) as a problem creator rather than a problem solver. Content that creates problems isn't as useful as content that solves problems. The former might well be talked about, but it's far less likely to be shared, and unlikely to be linked to and recommended.

Personality and voice

Having cautioned against confusing the public and private, I'm not advertising a ban on bringing your personality into the content. Positive self-reflection that shows your audience how you offer solutions makes for engaging and useful content.

One of the reasons I so enjoy Liz Jones's EAT SLEEP EDIT REPEAT blog is because she teaches me different ways of *thinking* and *doing* through the lens of her own experiences – often using personal anecdotes to ground her writing, but never losing sight of her professional audience and what they might want to learn from her. I associate this kind of strong, thoughtful writing with Liz – in my mind, it's part of her brand.

Credibility

The content you create as part of added-value marketing must be credible, otherwise it could damage your reputation rather than enhancing it. Certainly, it might still put you top of your target audience's mind, but for all the wrong reasons. Furthermore, it won't be shared, linked to, and recommended, which is a poor SEO strategy.

Quality control

If your content marketing is in written form, do the necessary quality control. If you're writing blog posts targeted at colleagues and those articles regularly confuse *its* and *it's*, use comma splices, and contain myriad spelling and grammar errors, no one in your community will trust you with a referral. That's an example of top of mind for the wrong reasons.

Test

If it's a widget, tool, macro, template or video, make sure the content works, otherwise it won't be of use and will therefore not be shared, linked to, or recommended.

Verify

If it's written advice, does it make sense? There's nothing wrong with putting forward advice that goes against the grain, but can you support the alternative position you're taking?

If I were to write a marketing booklet for colleagues that had a chapter on testimonials, and I stated that I thought these were not trusted by clients, difficult to acquire and therefore probably not worth the effort, my advice would be rejected by my alpha audience as nonsense; there is overwhelming evidence that the opposite is true, and my assertions in the booklet would serve only to undermine my professional reputation – that's negative marketing and needs to be avoided, so do carry out the wider reading and research before you publish.

7. Content marketing in action

Overview

In this section, I'll show you some examples of content marketing in the editorial community. It's a tiny selection but with it I hope to demonstrate that there are many different ways to add value.

The tool: Journal Selector

Journal Selector has been developed by Cofactor's Anna Sharman. Anna runs a scientific publishing consultancy based in London, UK, offering a range of editorial services to researchers, institutes and universities.

It's a free online tool that helps scholars decide which journals to submit their papers to based on criteria such as speed of publication, subject area and peer-review process.

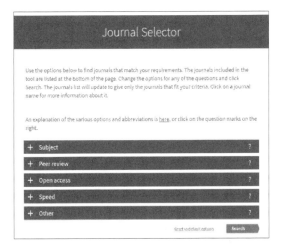

The blog: The Editing Blog

I set up The Editing Blog in 2011 with the aim of assisting primarily new entrants to the field with the business aspects of editorial freelancing. Over time, I've extended the reach to more to include independent fiction authors and fiction editors seeking to hone their line craft. The content I create on that blog reflects these audiences. I'm based in the UK, but the readership is global.

The tutorial: 'Microsoft Word Styles'

'Microsoft Word Styles' is a video tutorial created by Katherine Trail of KT Editing Services, based in Aberdeen, Scotland. The video was produced using on-board computer tools, so didn't cost Kat anything. It's professionally presented, easy to follow and useful for Kat's colleagues and potential clients.

The resource hub: Copyeditors' Knowledge Base

KOK Edit's Copyeditors' Knowledge Base is curated by US medical editor Katharine O'Moore-Klopf and is arguably the most comprehensive repository of editorial freelancing information available on the planet. It's considered a must-visit resource by everyone I know in the editorial community.

The advice hub: LinkedIn Learner Lounge

In the LinkedIn Learner Lounge, John Espirian shares all his experience about how to use LinkedIn as a visibility and lead-generation tool. John includes tons of free content, but there are also two paid-for option for those who need tailored consultations.

The podcast: The Editing Podcast

Denise Cowle and I launched our podcast in 2019. Our target audiences are professional editors and writers of fiction and non-fiction. The aim? To make people's editing and writing lives easier. We broadcast in seasons and regularly feature guests with specialist knowledge.

The booklet: Self-editing Your Novel

Developmental editor Sophie Playle offers this free booklet on her website as a way of demonstrating her skills, engaging with potential clients, and building her email list.

The conversation: CIEP annual conference, Aston, 2016

Here's me hanging out with some friends at an editing convention. The uppermost yellow arrow is pointing at my colleague Victoria Woodside from Northern Ireland (I'm left of her). The inset picture features editor Sophie Playle (mentioned above), who's based in England. These two women, in conversation, helped me to unpick my business, and tweak the service definitions on my website so that they speak more clearly to my target audience of independent authors – and all without compromising my existing brand.

My colleagues put themselves top of my mind such that I referred work to them. These valuable conversations took place in a bar and a pizzeria – content marketing doesn't have to be dull!

More client-focused examples of content marketing

Here are some additional examples of content marketing in action. These all have one thing in common: the content is aimed specifically at those who might commission editorial services – our clients.

- **'What's the Difference Between Developmental Editing, Content Editing, Copy Editing, and Proofreading?'**: This is one of several YouTube videos produced by Stacey Aaronson, a professional book doctor who specializes in working with independent authors. Check out the distinctive retro music and artwork!
- *How to Write Dialogue that Pops*: This is one of my own booklets. It's a 80-page PDF that helps newbie writers write compelling dialogue based on mood, voice and intention.
- **'The legal side of self-publishing'**: This blog article by Kate Haigh (KateProof) suggests some key legal themes that independent authors should investigate.

- **Editing Tips**: In this series of articles (available on writer Jami Gold's website), editor Naomi Hughes examines story, scene and writing craft issues that can trip up the beginner novelist and offers advice on how to fix these problems.
- Erin Brenner of Right Touch Editing has created several **PDF booklets** that aim to help authors 'edit better, work smarter, and publish more successfully': *Unraveling the Mysteries of Editors' Titles*, *How to Find the Right Editor* and *What Is Self-Publishing?*
- Melanie Austin, editor and owner of Seattle Editing, curates a **writers resource hub** on her website.

Ideas for content that you can use

Remember, if you want to create content that's specifically aimed at clients, think about the questions you've been asked (or that you might be asked).

If you're a new entrant to the editorial freelancing field, here's a list to get you going. These are some of the questions I've been asked over the past year and that could inspire (or already have inspired) content-based solutions.

- What's the difference between copyediting and proofreading?
- What are the pros and cons of writing under a pen name?
- I've commissioned a manuscript review. Is my book now ready for a final proofread – just to dot the i's and cross the t's?
- Where do I go to get my book cover designed?
- There are hundreds of references in my thesis. What's an efficient way to check that they're all included in my bibliography?
- The journal I'm submitting to wants me to style my references according to APA. I haven't a clue where to start.

- I'm a student – where's a good place to source full bibliographic information for my references?
- Structural, substantive, content, development, line and copyediting, and proofreading – what on earth is the difference between all of those and which ones do I need?
- You've told me what you recommend, but I can't afford all of that. What do I do? I want my book to be perfect!
- I'm a beginner writer. It is okay for me to self-publish now or should I wait until I'm more experienced?
- Do I need to commission any editing before I submit to an agent?
- I'm a student. To what degree can you help me? I worried about issues such as plagiarism and collusion.
- Which vanity presses are reputable and are the packages they're offering worth the money?
- My book's already been designed for print publication but I've only self-edited. I can give you a PDF. Can you do a thorough copyedit on it before I give the layout artist the go-ahead to print?
- I'm trying to get agent representation – what should I send them? The whole book, a few chapters and a letter, or something else?
- What's the ideal length of a novel?
- What's the average turnaround time for proofreading?
- I have a series of novels that need proofreading. Do you offer special pricing packages for bulk work?
- There's explicit sexual content in my book. Will it be difficult to find an editor or proofreader? Do I need to mention this when I ask for a quote?
- I need advice on marketing my self-published book. I know that's not your job but do you have any advice for me?
- My journal article needs tidying up. Does my editor need to have a higher-level degree in the subject area?

- I know you do proofreading and copyediting. Does this mean you can help me with characterization, pace, plot and structural issues as well?
- You've told me (gently) that I'm prone to repetition and word dump. Any advice on how I might tackle this?
- How many drafts should I write before I hire an editor?

All of these questions are problems for the clients who asked them. The answers are solutions and are therefore ripe for turning into superb useful content that you can use to promote your expertise to potential clients.

Doing the research

Even if you don't yet know the answers, there's nothing to stop you doing the research. Find out what those who do know are saying. Then incorporate that wealth of knowledge into your content.

Including the relevant attribution won't just benefit these experts – it'll also authenticate the information you've provided and, in the case of web-based content, create outbound links from your site to those whom you're citing (which is great for SEO).

Everyone wins – you, the expert, and the potential client.

8. How to build great content

Overview

In this chapter, I'll take you through the basics of building great content.

The most important thing to remember is that it's all about the customer. That's your starting point. If you make your content about you, you risk disengaging your audience, which means you could lose focus on where the value should be. And, as we now know, if there's no value, it's no longer content marketing – it's just stuff. That's a waste of your time.

The content-building framework

To ensure the content is customer-focused, take a look at the framework in the following table and consider the questions posed.

Content-building framework	
Goal	What's your business objective? What do you hope to achieve by creating the content?
Customer	Who is the customer you wish to engage with? Understanding who the customer is ensures your content stays on point.
Requirement	What does the customer want? What are their problems? If you understand the problems, your content can provide the solutions.
Interaction	What will the customer want/need to do with the content? Examples include reading it, watching it, listening to it, scribbling on it, highlighting portions of it, relaxing with it, scan-reading it, referring back to it, copying it, pasting it, taking reassurance from it.
Visibility	How will they find out about it? In other words, how will you make it discoverable

	for them? If they can't find it, it's of no use to them, no matter how great it is.
Delivery	How will you make it travel? For example, what format will it be in so that customers can access it (and share it) conveniently?
Verification	What are the alternative methods of delivering content and why did you not choose them? This helps you to ensure that the format you've chosen is the current best solution.
Alternatives	Are there other options that might consolidate your initial efforts further down the road? For example, you might create a booklet initially and, later, complement it with a video. Or a conversation might encourage you to create an information sheet.

Following are two case studies that show you how I used this framework to build two pieces of value-based content for two different audiences.

Case study 1: The digital proofreader

Here's how I answered the questions in the framework table.

Content-building framework: The digital proofreader	
Goal	To build a network with fellow proofreaders. I like working alone but not in isolation. To reduce the number of individual email queries I was receiving about proofreading on PDF.
Customer	Colleagues – primarily proofreaders working for publishers or other organizations supplying digital versions of typeset page proofs.

Requirement	Onscreen proofreading tools and instruction.
Interaction	See what it looks like in practice; try it on their own computers; learn how to use the tools; download relevant software or accessories.
Visibility	Discuss with colleagues at professional meetings; post information on a professional forum; deliver a course; create online resource hubs and blogs.
Delivery	Provide instructions and demos.
Verification	My colleagues would need the detail in written and visual formats. Infographics would be unable to include all the relevant information, and audio-only options, such as podcasts, wouldn't deliver vital visual cues.
Alternatives	Initial tools and the accompanying visual and written instructions could be supplemented with video, additional blog articles, a leaflet or small booklet, a presentation or course.

The solution

These are my digital BSI proof-correction stamps for PDF proofreading. I originally created them just for lil' ol' me, but realized that I could achieve two business goals if I went public with them.

I created information about the stamps on the blog of my website. I started with a post about how I use them and why they are useful. I included screenshots so that my colleagues could see what the tool looks like in practice. I included step-by-step written installation instructions. The post also included links to the relevant stamps files, which I'd uploaded to my website. These were, and still are, available to anyone, anywhere, at no charge.

I shared the blog post across my social media network and mentioned the files in discussions at my CIEP local-group meeting and on the CIEP forum.

I also sent a press release to the Publishing Training Centre and the publishers for whom I worked at the time.

Much later, I would follow up with a related guest article about onscreen proofreading for an online network with which I'm connected – BookMachine. I didn't know it at the time, but in 2017 BookMachine would partner with Kingston University Press to publish a book, *Snapshots*, about contemporary issues in publishing, and my article would be included.

I created a hub page on The Editing Blog that consolidates all the relevant links and files, along with sharing buttons to make it as easy as possible for my colleagues to access and share. There's also a button that links to this in the blog sidebar, which makes the tool accessible.

I added additional delivery methods as time went on, including a video tutorial that demonstrates installation that complements the original written instructions. There are already some great webinars demonstrating onscreen markup (for example, via my colleague Adrienne Montgomerie) so I'm not in a hurry to duplicate that content, even if I can put my own spin on it. I would, however, consider doing a presentation of the content in action at a conference workshop.

Case study 2: The indie author

Here's how I answered the questions in the framework table.

Content-building framework: The indie author	
Goal	To phase out my publisher work and expand the workflow from independent authors.
Customer	To increase income. I have more control over the prices I set my indie-author clients than I have over the prices I'm offered by publishers. I've found working directly with authors to be more lucrative so it's an effective way for me to earn more money for the same number of hours' work.
Requirement	To demonstrate my engagement with indie authors so that they feel compelled to hire me over my competitors.
Interaction	Independent authors of fiction and non-fiction.
Visibility	Self-editing tips and tools that will help them do some of the graft before commissioning an editor or proofreader.
Delivery	Read; copy and paste macros and find/replace strings to use in their own files; ask for guidance.
Verification	Google search; Twitter; writing workshops; visiting my website; via a course/workshop.
Alternatives	Downloadable information (or a link to it) that could be used in multiple online and offline settings. Being able to copy and paste the search strings would make the information convenient and easy to use.

The solution

I created a free PDF booklet called *The Author's Proofreading Companion*. It provides independent self-publishing writers with guidance on how to tidy up a Word document. The Companion includes some simple macros as well as a number of useful search strings for Word's find/replace and wildcard-search functions.

Authors can download it, copy and paste from it, look at examples and tweak them to suit their own needs, highlight their favourite tips, and refer back to it at will.

I blogged about it and shared the article via my social media network, which includes authors. I created a dedicated webpage under the 'Books and Guides' tab on my website. Here, I included information about what the booklet includes as well as the downloadable file.

In the future, I could develop the resource further by linking up with writers' workshops and courses in my region. I might also create some simple business cards that feature the cover of the booklet and a link to the download.

The content-building framework template

In the Appendix, I've included a template of the framework table. You can make as many copies of it as you wish – work through the questions to help you think through how you might create value-adding content for a dedicated customer group.

9. Using visual media

Overview

Visual elements (e.g. videos, slide shows, webinars, infographics, tables, images, photographs) serve a number of functions in content marketing. Before deciding which are best, let's break them down into three segments.

- **Moving:** videos, slide shows and webinars fall into this category. These are great for content that has an instructional element to it.
- **Static:** images, graphics and photographs make content eye-catching and recognizable. These are great for dense information that needs breaking up to prevent reader boredom and disengagement.
- **Informational:** examples include infographics and tables. These are useful for helping the customer to access complex content that needs a helping hand to make it digestible.

Ultimately, we want to maximize our audience's engagement. Using visual media can increase the chances of success because, according to developmental molecular biologist John Medina, (Brain Rules):

> Vision trumps all other senses … We are incredible at remembering pictures … If information is presented orally, people remember about 10%, tested 72 hrs after exposure. That number goes up by 65% if you add a picture.
> Pictures beat text as well, in part because reading is so inefficient for us.

Medina doesn't say we shouldn't use text but, rather, that we should enhance our text with useful images. Doing so will make our content memorable, which means the target audience is more likely to discuss, share, recommend and link to it, simply because it sticks in their minds.

To help you decide whether to include visual media – and if so, what types – consider the following questions:

- What else is **surrounding** your own content? Would visual elements help that content to stand out?
- What's **appropriate** given the nature of the valuable information you're providing?
- What are the audience's **preferences** – what do they want to do? This will vary so you might need to offer both the visual and the textual.
- Might including images build **trust**? Do the customers already know you and trust you, or are they new customers with whom you've still to prove your authenticity?
- Can you make your content more identifiable using visual media for **branding** purposes?

What else is surrounding your content?

This may be the biggest issue to consider when deciding whether to include visual media. According to Mark Schaefer in 'Content Shock':

> The amount of available web-based content (the supply) is doubling every 9 to 24 months … However, our ability to consume that content (the demand) is finite.

In other words, it's getting harder to be noticed, and to stand out from the crowd.

If you're delivering content into an environment that's already rammed to the hilt with other content, and the audience's attention span is limited, visual elements could be just what's needed to ensure that what you have to offer is visible and useful to them. Social media feeds are good examples. You could do a fantastic job of sharing your valuable stuff with all your followers, who in turn could do a fabulous job of sharing it to all of their followers.

But few in the Twitterverse have time to read every single tweet. Including images can make your tweets stand out and be noticed – as long as those images are useful in themselves.

What's appropriate?

The nature of the valuable information you're providing will determine your use of visual media.

If your content is long, complex, or contains information that some might think is boring, visual media could help to make it more digestible. The text will still be important because the information you're imparting requires explanation, but tables, infographics and summary-based images will make it easier on the eye.

Here are two superb examples of infographics that copywriter Tom Albrighton created to help freelancers visualize the pricing 'agreement zone' and the five stages of freelance pricing (ABC Copywriting).

Both of these images provide enough information to stand on their own, but if the reader does invest the time in reading the article, the detailed information that Tom's included will be much easier to understand because the infographics act as reference points that bring clarity to his discussion.

- If your content consists of short, snappy information bursts, custom images or screenshots might be more appropriate methods of delivery because they're easy to read and act on quickly.
- If your content is instructional, you might want to provide, say, video *and* text so that the user can learn what needs to be done, but also follow written instructions at their own pace once they come to the point of acting on your advice.

Broadly speaking, if visual media will bring clarity to your content, then including it is a must.

What are your audience's preferences?

Regardless of what *you* think is the best way to deliver content, be prepared for members of your audience to disagree! With that in mind, and the fact that the value for the customer is king, listen to feedback, especially from your alpha audience (see Visibility, above).

If you're big on video, but one of your core customer segments isn't engaging with it, step back and rethink. Some clients might enjoy reading substantive blog posts; others may prefer to just look at the infographic you've included within it – a quick-and-dirty option for the time-pushed reader. Some won't want to watch a video simply because they prefer to work through written instructions with screenshots. Different strokes for different folks.

Images and building trust

Do your customers already know you and trust you, or are they people with whom you've yet to prove your authenticity?

Research has shown that visual content boosts trust and social proof (see 'The Importance of Testimonials' and '7 Things You

MUST Understand When Leveraging Social Proof in Your Marketing Efforts'.

A supporting video, an anchoring mugshot, or a graphic that you've designed to complement written information could make the difference between whether a new customer engages with your content or moves on.

Using visual media to brand content

We've already discussed the sheer volume of content already available, and how it will continue to increase. Visual media can make our content more recognizable (see Identifiability, above). If it's identifiable as ours, and we're trusted, those in our network are more likely to share it, link to it, recommend it and talk about it.

Says logo designer John Williams ('The basics of branding'):

> Simply put, your brand is your promise to your customer. It tells them what they can expect from your products and services, and it differentiates your offering from your competitors'.

If you're interested in making your business more visible, consider how consistent use of images such as your face and your logo will enrich your content and enhance your brand. If you're not interested in making your business more visible, you're probably better off working for an employer than for yourself.

Choosing visual media – a quick guide

Here's a quick guide to help you consider the types of visual media you might integrate into your content marketing strategy. It's not the law – just a tool to get you thinking.

Quick Guide to Choosing Visual Media

Nature of your content

Complex, detailed
- **Options:** descriptive text
- **Support with:** infographic, screenshots

Information burst
- **Options:** static custom image with key message
- **Support with:** caption, business name or logo

Teaching tool/demo
- **Options:** video, screencast, webinar, slideshow
- **Support with:** written instructions+screenshots

What's surrounding your content

Lots – it's crowded
- **Options:** static custom image that features key message
- **Support with:** short description, caption, website address, hashtag or logo

You're the centre of attention
- **Options:** descriptive text
- **Support with:** static custom image, infographic, screenshot or video

Audience preferences

Ponder, copy, refer
- **Options:** descriptive text
- **Support with:** infographic, screenshots, static custom images

See in action
- **Options:** video, screencast, webinar, slide show
- **Support with:** written instructions

Quick glance
- **Options:** infographic
- **Support with:** caption, website address, business name or logo

Audience trust levels

Well known, high trust
- **Options:** descriptive text; audience more patient and knows it's worth reading
- **Support with:** relevant static images or moving visual media

Little known, lower trust
- **Options:** infographic, image of your face, relevant static custom images that feature key message, logo
- **Support with:** shorter descriptive text

Branding opportunities

Yes, everywhere
- **Options:** logo, business name, website address, email address, image of your face, telephone number, colourway that matches your business's

No
- **Options:** are you absolutely sure there's no opportunity or reason to brand your content? If so, redesign the content or rethink your strategy

Effective visual content marketing in action

Here are three examples of visual content marketing in action from our very own editorial community. There are many more but three is enough to show us how visual media can be used to make content more accessible for the audience.

They show us how we can use visual media creatively and appropriately to stand out, respond to the audience preference, instil trust and enhance branding.

Denise Cowle: 'How much does a proofreader cost?'

In this example, Denise has used informational visual media to create engagement.

Denise wrote a blog article explaining what proofreading costs and why. A key point was that cheap doesn't equate to value for money. The article targets potential clients, though new entrants to the editorial freelancing field would also find the information useful when thinking about how they talk to their own customers about pricing.

The information she presented was complex and needed detailed explanation. Some of her readers would be shoppers (clients using the web to source quotes from a range of suppliers) and their attention span might be limited. For that reason, she included a valuable infographic.

Hundreds of versions of the 'Good–Fast–Cheap: Pick Two' infographic are available for free online. There's a reason why it's been so widely reproduced – it's excellent. Denise thought so too and showed wisdom in using it.

- The simplicity of the infographic illustrates her key point perfectly, though the detail is provided in the text for those who want it.
- It provides enough clarity and understanding to enable it to stand on its own.
- It's memorable. I've read hundreds of blogs since Denise wrote her article, but her piece immediately sprung to mind as I was writing this book, and all because of that infographic.

Louise Harnby: The Editing Blog

In this example, I've has used static visual media to create engagement.

I regularly write detailed articles on my blog targeted at potential clients and colleagues. The text is long and demands the reader pay attention. I know that not all of the people reading my blog will already know me – I might not yet have built enough social proof with some members of my audience such that my content is perceived as honest and authentic.

Every blog entry is thus branded with an inset image. The design of the image is consistent across my articles.

- The images are eye-catching and break up the detailed text.
- They're not stock images, though – each one is customized for the post it's attached to. That customized message

reminds readers why they should invest their time in reading the detail – in other words, I show my audience what's in it for them.

- Because the design is consistent, it reinforces my brand, helping readers to easily identify the content as mine. This builds authenticity and trust.

John Espirian: #MicroMacTips

In this example, John has used informational visual media to create engagement.

John, a specialist technical writer, regularly delivers content to his customers using video and social media. I'm going to focus on his Twitter engagement here. Visit Twitter and type #MicroMacTips into the search box and you'll see how he's used his feed to create added value for his audience in the form of screenshots and custom-built images.

John has understood that the content he's providing can be acted on immediately. His audience doesn't need to ponder whether his tip is useful now or sometime in the future. If he tells them a useful keyboard shortcut, they'll want to start using it there and then.

Rather than relying on short textual descriptions of the shortcut that might get lost in the feed, he's used images to provide information bursts. And while the advice will be, or has already been, consolidated in and complemented by longer blog posts, booklets, demos or presentations, using visual bursts enables John to make his content highly visible and usable right now.

- John's understood that his content is surrounded by other content – and a vast amount of it at that. Most tweets are text-based. John's visual bursts therefore stand out and catch the eye.
- He's created a one-stop-shop of useful content for Mac users. Because the content is instantly testable, it quickly builds his audience's trust in him as helpful, supportive, encouraging and competent. That's good for his brand and his business. Mac users are everywhere, and some of them will need technical writing services. Guess who'll be top of mind?

Ultimately, the more valuable the visual elements are in their own right, the more effective they are as a content-marketing tool.

I'm not saying don't use stock images on your blogs. I'm saying that the more usable those images are in terms of providing actual valuable content themselves, the more bang for the buck for the audience.

And the more value they find in your content, the more likely they are to remember it, talk about it and share it, all of which will enhance the visibility of your business.

10. When to do content marketing

Overview

Content marketing is a slow burn. It may take months, even years to see the results of your labour. Rather than thinking about it in terms of a to-do list, consider yourself a gardener.

A gardener tends and nurtures. First, the seeds are planted (our content-marketing creation). The garden looks bare until the seedlings bud (our network begins to take notice; our valuable content is discussed and shared). Those seedlings grow into saplings (our visibility increases as we rise to the top of people's minds and improve our search-engine rankings). Finally, the saplings mature into trees (we achieve our business goals).

Content marketing and other strategies compared

You want to target publishers: direct mail or cold-call marketing

You send a mailshot to 100 UK presses. Within a week or two you'll have responses. Some presses will say yes, some will say no, and some will put you on hold until they have space in their freelance lists.

Of course, many won't reply. But if your skills and experience are strong, and you communicate them effectively, there's a good chance you'll be on the way to building a client portfolio.

This is something you do perhaps once, twice or more, but however little or often you do it, you get almost immediate yes/no results.

You want to target students: directory advertising

You advertise in your national editorial society's directory. Its Google rankings are reasonable. You're on show and therefore in direct competition with many colleagues. You're also restricted to a degree as to what information you can include.

However, the directory is keyword searchable and if your keywords match a student's preferences, there's a good chance you'll appear in a much smaller filtered list. This is something you set up once and review at regular intervals to ensure the listing is up to date.

You might get immediate results, or you might not, but once the listing's up it's working for you and you could receive an offer to quote at any time.

You want to target independent authors: content marketing

You create numerous blog posts and several PDF checklists and guidance notes that will be useful to self-publishing writers. You share these across your extensive online network. They are linked to, talked about, shared and recommended by colleagues (who want to provide resources for their own client network) and by existing and potential author clients within your network.

You might be lucky and get an almost immediate referral, though I'd recommend not counting on this. More likely, the impact will be on your Google rankings, but this will take time and regular application on your part in terms of delivering fresh content.

Google's like a giant directory, much bigger than the national society's directory, and with much more competition. However, because the competition is spread over a much bigger list, if you can get near the top you'll stand out more.

Time frames compared

- Direct-mail marketing is a quick-fix strategy
- Directory advertising is a gradual-fix strategy
- Content marketing is long-term strategy

None is better or worse than the others; they're just different. I recommend a broad marketing strategy that encompasses all three. Marketing that uses multiple tools across multiple platforms to target multiple client preferences is more likely to generate work leads that will help you develop your business and achieve your goals.

Avoiding fixation on the wrong thing

Ultimately, content marketing is an organic way of marketing. It's about taking a down-the-road approach to one's business that aims to increase visibility and maximize choice.

Fixating on *when* to do content marketing can lead us to **lose focus on value**, and value, lest we forget, is the most important principle underpinning the strategy.

It doesn't matter how often you create content. If that content isn't considered useful, it won't travel. It'll be static, forgettable. That's not content marketing – it's just stuff. And stuff won't put you top of mind (in a positive way) or top of Google. Neil Patel, in 'Get Back to Reality: 9 Content Marketing Expectations Busted', concurs:

> The reality is that you should focus on perfecting the art of producing better quality content that helps your audience. If you're just focusing on quantity then you're going to miss the mark on quality.

By all means, commit to blogging once a week. But make sure that every post is valuable – that people think the information contained within it presents you as credible, professional and full of useful advice or guidance. If you don't have anything useful/valuable to blog about – if the information you're blogging about doesn't compel people to think of you as a go-to, an expert, a professional who has solutions to offer – step back and wait. Then, when you do have value to offer, start posting again.

11. Revisiting the industry definitions

Overview

Early in this guide, I offered a simple definition of content marketing to help nervous marketers get their heads round the concept. Now let's revisit the industry definitions and break them down based on what we've learned.

Industry definition #1

> Content marketing is a strategic marketing approach focused on creating and **distributing valuable**, **relevant**, and **consistent** content to attract and retain a **clearly-defined audience** – and, ultimately, to drive profitable **customer action**. *(Content Marketing Institute)*

- **Distributing:** great content needs to be shared, otherwise it's static. To be shared, it needs to be visible so we need to be connected. See: 'Visibility'.
- **Valuable:** we've talked about usefulness and value throughout, but in particular see: 'For whom is it valuable?' and 'Underlying principles: Value'.
- **Relevant:** this is about putting the customer first and asking, 'What would they find useful?'. See: 'For whom is it valuable?', 'Working out what's useful', and the examples in 'How to build great content', in particular the questions 'Who is the customer?' and 'What do they want?'.
- **Consistent:** here we're talking about how content is presented so that it's identified with you and your business. See: 'Identifiability'.
- **Clearly-defined audience:** we're back again to the customer, and how we create our useful stuff around a

particular customer's problems. See: 'For whom is it valuable?', 'Working out what's useful', and the examples in 'How to build great content'.

- **Customer action:** this is a rather businessy way of saying goal or outcome. All of our goals will differ. Some of us might want to increase our workflow; others may want to acquire the same amount of work but from different client types; yet others might be looking for an income increase. See: 'Your business and its goals', 'Top of mind' and 'Top of Google'.

In fact, we can rewrite the CMI's definition in plainer language.

Content marketing = creating and delivering useful stuff for specific clients that's identifiable as ours and meets our goals.

Industry definition #2

Content marketing is the discipline of creating **quality branded** editorial content across **all media channels and platforms** to deliver engaging **relationships**, **consumer value** and **measurable success** for brands. *(Content Marketing Association)*

- **Quality:** I like the fact that the CMA includes this component in its definition. Low quality means low credibility. Content that's poor on credibility is more likely to damage than enhance our chances of achieving our goals. See: 'Credibility'.
- **Branded:** as with the CMI definition, this asks us to consider how the content is presented so that it's identified with you and your business. See: 'Identifiability'.
- **Media channels and platforms:** here we're being asked to consider how we make the content available to whomever we want to access it. See: 'Visibility', 'Usability' and 'Different types of content marketing'.

- **Relationships:** this invites us to acknowledge who the customer is and what they want, and reminds us that content marketing stretches beyond the physical – it's about engaging people and being a regular human being. See: 'For whom is it valuable?', 'Underlying principles: Value', 'Working out what's useful', and the examples in 'How to build great content', 'Top of mind', 'Being human' and 'The conversation'.

- **Consumer value:** this is about the customer and what they want – how the content is relevant. See: 'For whom is it valuable?', 'Underlying principles: Value', 'Working out what's useful', and the examples in 'How to build great content', in particular the questions 'Who is the customer?' and 'What do they want?'.

- **Measurable success:** yet another way of saying goal or outcome. See: 'Your business and its goals', 'Top of mind' and 'Top of Google'.

Let's rewrite it in plainer language, just so we know we're on the same page with the CMA.

> Content marketing = creating high-quality useful stuff that's identifiable as ours, visible, creates engagement with specific clients, and meets our goals.

In fact, both those industry definitions are perfectly usable *and* useful now that we've found a comfort zone with the language and the key concepts.

12. Final words

I hope you've found this guide useful. It is, after all, an example of content marketing in its own right ... that is, *if* you've found value in it. If you have, perhaps you'll tell your colleagues about it. If you haven't, you certainly won't. Ultimately, the success of this book will come down to you because you're the customer – my target audience. If I haven't helped you, if I haven't offered you solutions to problems, then I've simply created stuff that won't be discussed, shared, linked to and recommended.

My goals were similar to those I had in mind when I created my proofreading stamps and made them available online: to engage with colleagues and provide answers to questions that I'm often asked. And, yes, I've made a few quid with each sale, too, so thank you.

Owning an editorial business requires thinking about our own business goals and what our customers – whether clients or colleagues – want and how we can help them. Content marketing is one way of doing that.

I won't pretend it doesn't require investment of your time – it does; all aspects of running a business require that. However, the rewards – top of mind and top of Google – can help you transform your business into one that offers you choice of what you earn, whom you work for and which services you provide.

Content marketing is, indeed, a slow burn, but that's no bad thing. No business owner lives in a vacuum of *now*. The future is always ahead of us, and knowing that the investment we make now, via value-added marketing, will have benefits that stretch well into that future is something to be embraced and nurtured.

I wish you well on your own content-marketing journey!

Appendix

Resources

- Andrew and Pete's website is a great place to go if you want to learn how to have huge amounts of fun with creating added value and making your business more interesting and discoverable. Take a look at their free videos and books on small-business marketing, plus a couple of paid-for tools: ATOMIC, a membership hub for those who want to learn about creating vibrant content, and their book, *Content Mavericks* (Andrew and Pete, 2017): https://www.andrewandpete.com.
- Blogging for Business Growth is my multimedia online course that will take you step by step through everything you need to know to build and sustain a blog: harnby.co/courses.
- Branding for Business Growth is my multimedia online course that helps you discover the flavour of you and build a unique brand identity: harnby.co/courses.
- Content Marketing Association (UK): http://the-cma.com.
- Content Marketing Institute (USA; includes a stack of useful articles, book recommendations, tips and templates: click on the Articles tab): http://contentmarketinginstitute.com.
- Donna Moritz, '25 Experts Share Top 3 Content Marketing Trends for 2017': http://writtent.com/blog/content-marketing-trends.
- *How to be visible with Social Media* (Business Skills for Editors series). This business-skills guide shows editors and proofreaders how to use social media to increase online visibility, expand their audience, reinforce brand and generate leads ... without falling into a rabbit hole and

without spending any money. It's the lite version of the multimedia course and excludes the supporting resources: harnby.co/books.

- *How to Brand Your Editing Business* (Business Skills for Editors series). This business-skills guide shows editors and proofreaders how to build an emotion-based brand identity that's rich in the flavour of you, and compelling to the people you'd love to work with. It's the lite version of the multimedia course and excludes the supporting resources: harnby.co/books.
- *How to Build an Editorial Blog* (Business Skills for Editors series). This business-skills guide shows editors and proofreaders how to create a captivating blog-based content platform that drives traffic to your website, makes you visible in the search engines, and adds value for your clients-to-be. It's the lite version of the multimedia course and excludes the supporting resources: harnby.co/books.
- John Medina, Brain Rules: http://www.brainrules.net/vision.
- John Williams, 'The basics of branding', https://www.entrepreneur.com/article/77408.
- Mark Schaefer is an internationally known marketer, speaker, author and consultant. His {grow} blog provides original thought-provoking insights into how you might use digital marketing to, you guessed it, grow your business. There's a book, too, for those who want to go deeper: *The Content Code* (Schaefer, 2015).
- Mark Schaefer, 'Content Shock': https://www.businessesgrow.com/2014/01/06/content-shock.
- Mark Schaefer, 'Driving economic benefits from your Alpha Audience': https://www.businessesgrow.com/2016/03/24/alpha-audience.

- *Marketing Your Editing & Proofreading Business* (Harnby, 2014). This is where to go if you want general advice on kick-starting your business's marketing strategy from the ground up. Like this guide, it's targeted specifically at editorial freelancers: harnby.co/books.
- Martin Huntbach, '7 Ways Content Marketing will Improve Search Engine Optimisation': https://www.thecontentmarketingacademy.co.uk/content-marketing-for-seo/#more-6573.
- Neil Patel, '7 Things You MUST Understand When Leveraging Social Proof in Your Marketing Efforts': https://neilpatel.com/blog/social-proof-factors-2/
- Neil Patel, 'Get Back to Reality: 9 Content Marketing Expectations Busted': http://contentmarketinginstitute.com/2017/01/content-marketing-expectations-busted.
- *Omnibus: Editorial Business Planning & Marketing Plus* (Harnby, 2016). The *Omnibus* is a PDF book that includes all of the content in *Marketing Your Editing & Proofreading Business*, *Business Planning for Editorial Freelancers*, and some additional bonus material: harnby.co/books.
- Sitepoint, 'The Importance of Testimonials', https://www.sitepoint.com/the-importance-of-testimonials.
- The Editing Blog – marketing-tips archive: http://www.louiseharnbyproofreader.com/blog-the-proofreaders-parlour/category/marketing tips.
- Tom Albrighton, 'The 5 Stages of Freelance Pricing': http://www.abccopywriting.com/2016/08/08/five-stages-freelance-pricing/

Content-building framework template

Content-building framework	
Goal	What's your business objective? What do you hope to achieve by creating the content?
Customer	Who is the customer you wish to engage with? Understanding who the customer is ensures your content stays on point.

Requirement	What does the customer want? What are their problems? If you understand the problems, your content can provide the solutions.
Interaction	What will the customer want/need to do with the content? Examples include reading it, watching it, listening to it, scribbling on it, highlighting portions of it, relaxing with it, scan-reading it, referring back to it, copying it, pasting it, taking reassurance from it.

Visibility	How will they find out about it? In other words, how will you make it discoverable for them? If they can't find it, it's of no use to them, no matter how great it is.
Delivery	How will you make it travel? For example, what format will it be in so that customers can access it (and share it) conveniently?

Verification	What are the alternative methods of delivering content and why did you not choose them? This helps you to ensure that the format you've chosen is the current best solution.
Alternatives	Are there other options that might consolidate your initial efforts further down the road? For example, you might create a booklet initially and, later, complement it with a video. Or a conversation might encourage you to create an information sheet.

Printed in Great Britain
by Amazon